PAPERS ON RAILWAY ENGINEERING, PREPARED BY GEORGE L. VOSE, FOR THE USE OF RAIL ROAD ENGINEERS.

NO. 10.

DESCRIPTION AND SPECIFICATION

OF A

NEW SYSTEM OF LOCOMOTIVE ENGINES

FOR RAILWAYS,

BY

GEORGE L. VOSE, CIVIL ENGINEER,

1854.

The Papers when complete will form a Volume of 200 pages octavo, containing all formulæ and instructions necessary for constructing the Roadbed, Stone, Iron and Wooden Bridges, Artificial Foundations, and other operations coming within the duty of the Railway Engineer. Price $1,00.

AUGUSTA:
RUSSELL EATON, PRINTER.
1854.

TO A. P. ROBINSON, Esq.,

Civil Engineer,

This paper is respectfully inscribed,

By his most ob't serv't,

GEORGE L. VOSE.

DIVISION OF THE SUBJECT.

Classification of Locomotives.

Of the Resistances.

Of the Power.

Description and Specification of the new Engine.

Comparison between the new and old Engines.

Conclusion.

LOCOMOTIVE ENGINES.

"When the magnitude of the capital invested in the locomotive stock of a Railroad, and the large portion of the annual revenue absorbed in maintaining it, are considered, its economical importance may be readily estimated."

LARDNER.

Railway machinery may be divided into two parts, fixed, and moving, and the moving subdivided into locomotive power, and carrying stock, or cars.

The moving power on a large Railway, should be arranged under three distinct heads.

Express passenger engines.

Ordinary passenger engines.

Freight engines.

First class locomotives for express passenger traffic, are required to draw light trains at extreme velocities, having a single pair of driving wheels of large diameter, low centre of gravity, to ensure steadiness, long wheel base, that the leading and trailing wheels may have great leverage to keep the engine on the rails, power of generating a large volume of steam of little density, in a short time, and such an arrangement of reciprocating machinery, that the rocking, rolling and twisting motions arising from this source, may be reduced to a minimum.

Second class engines, intended for ordinary passenger,

emigrant, way and mixed trains, moving from 25 to 40 miles per hour, and having two pairs of driving wheels, coupled.

Third class, freight locomotives, whose duty is the transport of heavy trains, at moderate velocities, i. e. from 10 to 12 miles per hour, these have three, four, and even five pair of driving wheels, coupled; the whole weight of the engine being available for traction, and consuming a moderate bulk of very dense steam.

The resistances to motion, the disturbing forces, and consequently the cost of working, increase in a much higher ratio than the speed, it is even supposed by some to increase as the square; express trains are most always run at a loss. It is stated that the London and North Western Railway, (England,) would save annually $100,000, by removing their expresses. The increased expense is not, though, entirely due the extra wear and tear from increased speed, but partly to the delaying of ordinary trains in motion at the same time; however, fast travelling being in some cases very desirable, it behooves us to render it as unobjectionable as possible.

The resistance to the motion of a railway train, may be divided as follows:—

Resistances of the train.

Resistances of the locomotive.

The resistance of the train is composed of

Friction,

Oscillation,

Atmospheric pressure.

FRICTION.

We distinguish here, axle and wheel friction; that of the axle is composed of two parts: the direct vertical friction on the journal, and the side friction on the collar, consequent upon lateral motion; the vertical friction is independent of the surface pressed, or of velocity, but is directly proportional to the pressure, and the same remark applies to that of the collars; as the diameter of wheel increases, the vertical action is lessened, but oscillation (the center of gravity being raised) being greater, lateral action is increased, the direct cause of the vertical is the weight of the car, and of the lateral, irregularities in the level of the surface of the rails.

Wheel friction (which acts between the periphery of the wheel and surface of rail,) increases with the load, and decreases with the increase of diameter of wheels.

The atmospheric pressure is not caused by direct action on the front and sides of the train, as might be supposed, but by the exhausting action in the rear, the train has, as it were, to pull along a large column of air—form or amount of frontage has little or no effect—the resistance depends on the bulk of the train.

NOTE. The following results on the resistances to Railway trains were obtained by Lardner, after extensive and careful experiments.

1st. That the great part of the resistance is due the atmosphere.

2d. That the shape of the front or back of the train, or spaces between the cars has no effect.

3d. That the same frontage offers more resistance as the bulk of the train increases.

The resistances to the motion of the locomotive may be divided into those of the carriage and of the engine.

CARRIAGE RESISTANCES.

The following motions may be perceived in a locomotive engine of the common construction while in motion, and the greater the velocity, the more strikingly are these developed. First—longitudinal swaying, arising from the alternate backward and forward motions of the piston-rods, cross-heads and connections. Second—a pitching of the engine upon the driving axle, as a fulcrum, caused by the vertical action of the cross-heads on the guide-bars. Third—a rocking laterally, arising from the longitudinal difference of position of the cross-heads, one acting on the centre of the guides, with its greatest vertical action, while the other acts at the end with its least. Fourth—twisting motion, owing to the angular position of the cranks, which act together during the first quarter revolution, opposed in the second, together in the third, and opposed in the fourth.

These movements must be opposed as follows: longitudinal swaying by counterbalancing the wheels opposite the crank-pins. Pitching and rocking, by placing the cylinders in such a position that the guide-bars shall be under the heaviest part of the engine, whereby they have more weight opposed to the cross-head action, and by increasing the wheel-base to give the leading and trailing wheels more leverage on the mass of the engine.

ENGINE RESISTANCES.

These are friction of pistons, cross-heads, side-valves, cranks, eccentrics and pumps, and compressed steam in the cylinder. The back pressure of the blast is a trifling resistance to that which exists during the escape of the compressed steam. Loss by condensation and priming during the passage of steam from the boiler to the cylinder may also be classed as a resistance, as it is a source of waste. Unequal admission of steam to the two ends of the cylinder, arising from the difference of the central positions of the piston and crank, caused by the angularity of the latter, results in a variation of pressure during the forward and backward stroke, which causes longitudinal swaying. This is corrected by varying the lap of the two ends of the valve.

The formula for the total resistance to the motion of any locomotive, with any load, upon any grade, at any velocity, is

$$R = \frac{E\left(\frac{V}{2} + 5 + (V^2 \cdot T \cdot 00004) + (V^2 \cdot B \cdot 00002) + \frac{V\,T}{15} + 6\,T\right.}{E + T} + G \quad (A)$$

Where E = weight of the engine and tender.

V = velocity in miles per hour.

T = weight of the train in tons.

B = bulk of the train in cubic feet.

G = resistance in lbs. per ton due gravity on an incline, found by multiplying 2240 by the fraction expressing the inclination and R = the resistance in lbs. per ton.

An example will show the use of the formula.

Let the engine and tender weigh 20 tons.

Call the velocity 50 miles per hour,

the weight of the train 100 tons,

the bulk of the train 50,000 cubic feet,

and assume G = 0, or the road level, the formula becomes,

$$R = \frac{20\left(\frac{50}{2} + (2500 \times 100 \times \cdot 00004) + (2500 \times 50000 \times \cdot 00002) + \frac{50 \times 100}{15} + 600\right.}{120} = 42$$

very nearly. 42 lbs. to each ton weight of the engine and train is the total resistance, and if the engine is capable of exerting a traction of 4200 lbs., it will draw 100 tons at 50 miles per hour on a level.

The results obtained from the formulae in this paper are perfectly reliable, as they are deduced from the extended and varied experiments made by Gooch (the Superintendent of the locomotive department of the Great Western Rail-road, England) and verified by the rules given in Clarke's Railroad Machinery; the calculated amounts of friction and other resistances given by the formulae are found to agree exactly with those obtained by the dynanometer.

OF THE POWER.

The fuel at the furnace grate, is the agent which raises the power in the boiler which, exerted in the cylinder, and transferred to the circumference of the driving wheel, serves to move the engine and its load. The steam-generating and consuming powers of the engine, and its adhesion, are the elements which determine its ability to perform any amount of work. *Traction* is the power exerted in the cylinder referred to the circumference of the driving wheel. *Adhesion* is the medium through which this is rendered available. *Traction* is governed by the dimensions of cylinder, steam pressure, and diameter of wheels. *Adhesion* by the weight of engine, the number and diameter of wheels, and the grade of the road.

The tractive power of an engine of any dimensions is expressed by

$$\frac{(PA)\,2S}{C}$$

when p = pressure in lbs. per square inch,
a = area of piston,
s = stroke in feet,
c = circumference of driving wheel in feet,

and

$$\frac{\frac{(PA)\,2S}{C}}{R} = W \quad \text{- - - - - - - -} \quad (B)$$

When R= the resistance in lbs. found by formula (A,) and W= weight in tons which the engine can carry.

From the formulae A and B the following tables are calculated, showing the effect of grades, load and velocity upon locomotion.

TABLE 1.

Velocity being constant, as also the expenditure of power,

the load on a level being			1000 tons
that on a 25 foot grade is			800 "
"	50	"	656 "
"	60	"	616 "
"	70	"	570 "
"	80	"	540 "

TABLE 2.

The load being constant, and velocity on a level			50 miles per hour.
that on a	25	foot grade is	37 "
"	50	"	30 "
"	60	"	27 "
"	70	"	25 "
"	80	"	23 "

From whence it appears that in traversing an ascent, we must reduce either the load or the speed, the expenditure of power remaining the same; if the velocity is reduced at this point, it must be correspondingly increased at other portions of the line to maintain an average speed, or if we decrease the load, we must traverse the grade twice, or have recourse to a grade engine; in either case we work at an economical disadvantage. The great desideratum in such cases, (and they occur on every Railway,) is power to graduate the force of the engine according to the work to be done; to be sure, the action of the steam upon the piston can be somewhat governed by the variable expansion gear, this effects the *traction* but not the *adhesion*, the sand box is the only expedient which has been adopted with effect thus far, and the evil arising from such an application is too palpable to need remark.

First Class Express Passenger Locomotive.

DESCRIPTION.

My improvements in first class engines have for their object the attainment of very high velocities, (from 75 to 100 miles per hour,) with a greater degree of steadiness than would be possible in the present construction. For this purpose I first reduce the centre of gravity from 8 to 4 feet above the rails, by placing two locomotives of the common construction, but of somewhat smaller dimensions than generally used, head to head upon the same track; both exhausting into a common smoke-box, through which passes the driving axle—thus the diameter of wheel has no effect upon the height of centre of gravity. The best mode of reducing the centre of gravity that has been applied thus far, is Crampton's English patent, in which the driving axle is placed behind the fire-box; but owing to their great wear upon the rails, caused by so large a flanged guiding wheel, the engine was laid one side. 2d. I place the cylinders, four in number, on the sides of the two fire-boxes, and protect them completely from the cold air. The steam-pipes are led from the dome, which is placed over the fire-box, through a heated casing outside, or by a common pipe passing inside the inner fire-box—by which condensation is prevented during the passage of the steam. By the same arrangement, the guides are placed under so great a weight as effectually to resist vertical action from the cross-heads; both ends of the engine are supported on trucks, and the driving-wheels being without flanges, the passage of curves is perfectly easy—the long wheel base effectually prevents rocking. The use of four cylinders saves the necessity of large machinery, which a single pair of equal area would require, and reduces the steam pressure to one half what it would be, were one pair of the small size used, with the same consumption of water. The blast is produced by a jet of steam drawn directly from the boiler, and regulated by a valve in the hands of the engine driver. The fire may thus be kept at any desired rate of combustion, both during motion and while the engine is stationary. By this arrangement we are enabled to use the strongest blast when we most need it, i. e. when ascending long grades. In the common construction the blast decreases as this requirement increases. The steam in the cylinders is worked expansively and then discharged into the open air. This arrangement is adopted on account of the great distance of the cylinders from the smoke-box—the steam would require too early a release to act with sufficient force for effective blast after so long a passage. The best way of showing the superiority of this construction over the old one, is by a comparison of dimensions of the two to perform a given amount of work. Suppose we are required to draw 100 tons at a velocity of 100 miles per hour, the height of centre of gravity being kept thesame in both the corresponding dimensions, are as follows:

	New Engine.	*Common construction.*
Diameter of wheel,	11 ft. 4 in.	11 ft. 4 in.
Cylinders,	16 in.	24 in.
Stroke,	2 ft.	2 ft.
Pressure,	120 lbs.	120 lbs.
Reduction,	10 per ct.	20 per ct.
Cut off,	75	75
Length of boiler,	20 ft.	66 ft.
Evaporating surface,	3000 sq. ft.	3300 sq. ft.

and the length of the boilers being kept the same, the heights of centres of gravity above the rail are 8 and 11 feet, and the gauge being 6 feet, the relative stability is expressed by 48 to 66.

As the difficulty of stopping a train increases at the same time with the speed, it becomes necessary to alter the commonly used brake, and accordingly I have applied brakes by a powerful system of levers to the driving wheels, the force acting equally and simultaneously from the frame upon both sides of the wheel, that the axle guards shall receive no strain.

The following specification gives a general idea of the arrangement of the new locomotive.

FRAME.

The frame to be of the best wrought iron, passing inside the wheels and bolted to both fire-boxes, the expansion machinery for both engines to be at the common smoke-box. At the fire-boxes the frame will be double—the parallel bars being at such a distance apart as to furnish a suitable bed for the cylinders, steam chests, &c., the base of the engine, from which all is made, is to be this frame. Particular care must be taken to connect the cylinders and the bearing of the driving wheels, as the whole force of the engine is exerted alternately one way and the other, between these points; the frame to be so arranged behind the rear fire-box as to give the draw-link power of acting directly thereon, *it* (the link) being entirely unconnected with the furnace; the bearing of the engine upon the driving-wheels is to be inside the latter, the connection being outside. The axle-guards, boxes, springs, &c. to be of the most approved construction. The trucks (one at each end) will have 4 wheels each, with out-side bearings. All of the bogie wheels will be flanged; the diameter 4 feet; wrought iron with 2 inch tires; axle hollow, 4 inches in diameter, of half inch iron.

DRIVING WHEELS,

Of wrought iron, spokes, nave and rim, with steel tire; the spokes to be one foot apart at circumference; diameter of wheel* 11 feet 4 inches at the tread of tire, without a flange. (NOTE. This diameter is for a velocity of 100 miles per hour. It is obtained as follows: from experiments made on the Great Western Railroad, (England,) it appears that 72 miles per hour is the maximum speed to which an engine with 8 feet wheels can attain, under the most favorable

---

*As there is an idea prevailing that the centrifugal force increases rapidly with the diameter of the wheel, I take this opportunity to compare a 6 and 10 foot driver.

The weight of the first is	1800 lbs.
That of the second	2000 lbs.
At the same velocity of engine, the centrifugal force of the first is	250,000 lbs.
And of the second,	250,000 lbs.

Diameter, therefore, need not be considered, in point of safety.

circumstances, the resistance to increased velocity being unbalanced machinery, slide valves, steam compressed in the cylinder, &c. Now 72 miles per hour with 8 foot wheels is 253 strokes of piston per minute. This is the utmost speed to be attained by the machinery; and increased velocity of the engine can be got only by an increased diameter of wheel. Thus have we been led to adopt the diameter named above.) The driving axle bears only upon two points, i. e. the frame bearings. It may be confined laterally by frame plates, but not vertically.

MACHINERY.

The connecting rods, pump-rods, guide bars, &c., &c., are all to be hollow, and of sufficient thickness to give the requisite strength; all bushes, screws, eccentric rods, oil cups, and small machinery to be made after the most approved pattern, the valve motion to be independent of the link.

FIRE-BOXES.

These to be made of copper of suitable thickness, the sides being slightly inclined to give free escape to the steam, the outer shells to be of the best rolled iron, and so connected with the barrels as to be perfectly tight.

BARRELS.

To be of cylindrical form, 12 feet extreme length, and 5 feet diameter, inside, to be supplied with the proper number of brass tubes, and so stayed as to resist the pressure to which they will be subjected.

The steam pipes are to be led through a heated passage to prevent condensation; the cocks, safety-valves and levers for working the machinery, to be made after the best models.

All parts of boilers, steam-pipes, cylinders, &c., to be protected by a jacket or by felting.

This engine is accompanied by two engine-drivers, and two firemen; the rear tender carries the tank with a supply of water for both boilers.

Second Class Locomotive Engines for Ordinary Passenger Traffic.

The objects to be attained here are increased power, greater steadiness, and greater safety than ordinary engines afford, these are accomplished by the use of 3 cylinders, two being placed at the fire-box, and one in the smoke-box, this latter gives the blast, the first two work in precisely similar positions, the third acts as a compensator, being placed at right angles to the others, the two are outside connected, the one inside, the forces thus act directly backward and forward without the side motion seen in the ordinary engine; the use of three cylinders gives more power without a proportional increase of expense; there are two pair of driving wheels coupled, of 6, 7 or 8 feet diameter, and made of wrought iron; both of these pairs are without flanges, the engine is kept on the rails by a four-wheeled truck in front, and by a single set of trailing wheels behind.

Third Class Engines for the Transport of Freight.

These engines have five pairs of driving-wheels of cast iron, with chilled tires, upon which the whole weight rests, two fire-boxes, and two barrels of large diameter; four cylinders arranged as in the first class locomotive, wheels four feet in diameter, the front and back pairs only being flanged, the connection is outside, valve motion obtained from the link, fire-boxes and boilers of the simplest construction; weight of largest engines for heavy trains 50 tons, maximum power at 120 pounds per square inch, 2000 tons on a level at 15 miles per hour, or, 1000 tons on an 80 foot grade.

COMPARISON OF OLD AND NEW ENGINES.

First as regards the Equating of Grades.

"The problem of the equation of grades, depends not only upon their disposition and direction, with reference to heavy traffic, but also upon the capacity of motive power.

ZERAH COLBURN."

Making the consumption of steam the point upon which the matter hinges, *capacity* of motive power might seem to have no part in the equation, as a certain amount of power is required to produce a given effect, but considering the *number* and *mileage* of engines, it has a bearing, and a very decided one, and it is upon these last elements that the depreciation of permanent way and the majority of repairs depend.

As an example of the equating of grades by locomotives of different capacity, let us take the New York and Erie Railroad. From a recent report it appears that the same power will draw—

16	cars on the	Western division,
40	"	Susquehanna,
25	"	Delaware, and—
14	"	Eastern.

The ruling grade on the Susquehanna division is 10 feet per mile, equal to one-third the resistance on a level, so four-thirds of 40 or 53, is the equivalent load on a level; the horizontal lengths corresponding to the several divisions are then as follows:—

Western	$127 \times \frac{53}{16} = 421$
Susquehanna	$140 \times \frac{53}{40} = 185$
Delaware	$104 \times \frac{53}{25} = 220$
Eastern	$74 \times \frac{53}{14} = 280$

The whole length by actual measurement is 445 miles, and by equating as above 1106.

Now suppose, by varying the power of the locomotive, we are enabled to take 40 cars over the entire length of the road, we shall equate as follows:—

Western	$127 \times \frac{53}{40} = 168$
Susquehanna	$140 \times \frac{53}{40} = 185$
Delaware	$104 \times \frac{53}{40} = 138$
Eastern	$74 \times \frac{53}{40} = 98$

Here the difference between the equated and actual distance, is but 144 miles, while by the system above it is 562, the difference of which two last is 418 miles, which is the length of horizonal line gained by increased capacity of motive power, thus the road is only 144 miles longer by equated than by actual distance, or 32 per cent., while by the present mode of operation, it is shown by its practical working to be 87 1-2 per cent., this then saves 55 1-2 per cent. of the equated mileage.

Comparison as to Working Expenses.

The items of expenses are:—

Cost of maintaining the way,	A
Repairs of locomotives,	B
Engine and train hands,	C
Fuel and cost of preparing,	D
Oil for engines,	E

The proportion of these items to the total cost of working, are from actual result of the Erie and Baltimore and Ohio engines as follows:

Cost of moving 222 tons of freight over the Erie Railroad, in the year 1852.

A	$12,19
B	7,52
C	12,70
D	13,87
E	2,19
All other expenses,	25,32
Total,	$73,79

And on the Baltimore and Ohio Railroad for the same year, the following are the proportions of these items:—

A	.295
B	.104
C	.094
D	.036
E	.161
	.690
All other expenses,	.243
Total,	.933

The engines of these two roads are of the following dimensions, the guage of the Erie being 6 feet, and that of the Baltimore and Ohio 4 feet 8 1-2 inches.

Erie.	B. and O.	
63000 lbs.	57400 lbs.	Total weight.
42000 "	57400 "	Weight on drivers.
18X20	20X22	Cylinders.
60 in.	43 in.	Wheels.

At the same steam pressure, the Baltimore exerts 90 per cent. more power than the Erie, and adding to this the mechanical advantage of the reduced guage, we may consider the former as acting with double the power of the latter, and the practical operation of the two roads show that they act up to this.

The expenses tabulated above, amounting to 75 per cent. of the total cost of transport, are not proportional to the capacity of engine or train, but depend almost entirely upon the *number* and *mileage* of the engines, in fact the repairs of the Baltimore engines for 1853 averaged $1,254 each, and those of the Erie $1,924, notwithstanding the severer grades and curvature of the former.

The expenses of engine and train employees are of course proportional to the number of trains run.

The capital invested in *fixed*, depends also on the amount of rolling stock.

It is not enough to take into account mileage alone in comparing light and heavy engines, as the latter would do a great deal more work on the same length of road, and consequently earn more.

If a heavy engine will work 1000 tons on a 60 foot grade, while the light one will draw the same amount on a level only, then is the *number* of trains reduced from 3 to 1, supposing a 60 foot grade to absorb 3 times the power necessary on horizontal road. As the *number* of trains run decreases, so does liability to accident, and necessity of moving fast. As the speed decreases, so does the resistance, and in a very rapid ratio. The velocity by which the maximum useful effect is obtained from freight engines, is from 10 to 15 miles per hour.

Application of New Engines to Massachusetts Western R. R.

The length from Worcester to Albany is 156 miles; the total rise and fall 3500 feet. Of the whole length, 23 miles are on grades from 50 to 83 feet per mile, and 88 of the remainder above 30 feet. The most difficult part of the road to work economically, is from Springfield to Pittsfield. Here the steepest grades occur. The freight engines in commonest use on this road are of the following dimensions:

Cylinders,	15X20
Wheels,	4 to 5 ft.
Whole weight,	56,000 lbs.
" on each wheel,	9,300 lbs.

Consumption of steam 3481 c. ft. per mile; adhesion 2-9ths the weight on driving wheels. 130 tons is the maximum load which can be taken over the 83 foot grades. (See American R. R. Journal for Feb. 18, 1854.)

The daily freight train from Springfield to Albany is divided into three parts while overcoming the principal summit; each of these parts is taken by an engine which, by exerting itself to the utmost, is able (sometimes without but generally with the use of sand) to surmount the ascent. Now the power of these engines upon the 83 foot grade being 130 tons, to move 1040 tons from Springfield to Pittsfield would require eight engines. With a freight locomotive built according to the new system, this 1040 tons may be easily taken at 10 or 15 miles per hour by an engine of the following dimensions:

Weight,	50 tons.
Weight on each wheel.	5 tons.
No. of wheels,	10
Diameter of wheels,	4 feet.
Cylinders,	21 X 24
Steam pressure,	120

15,886 cubic feet of steam per mile.

The mileage is thus reduced from 400 to 50 miles, (calling the distance 50 miles*—the exact length I have not at hand,) and the number of trains from eight to one. The cost of maintenance arising from depreciation of superstructure by the locomotive, depends upon the mileage. This, in the case before us, is reduced 7-8ths. The cost of locomotive power is as the number of engines running. As the new Engine has nearly double the machinery and boilers of the common construction, it must be considered as amounting in cost of repairs, attendance, &c., to twice as much as a single locomotive. The reduction of expense of engines is then 3-4, and the whole gain

$$7\text{-}8 + 3\text{-}4 = 13\text{-}8 = 162\ 1\text{-}2 \text{ per cent.};$$

or in dollars and cents—each engine costing $30 per day, and train hands $10—the amount at present would be $320, and by the new system $70 per day—the difference being $250 per day, or $90,000 per ann. saved on engine and train, to which add 7-8ths the annual cost of track repairs, equal to about $30,000, and 3-4ths the cost of fuel, $20,000 more, and we have the whole gain, $150,000, on freight alone, which employs a capital of $2,500,000, that might otherwise be expended on the permanent way, or distributed among the stockholders.

* From Springfield to Pittsfield.

CONCLUSION.

EXPRESS TRAINS.

By use of the new locomotive, express passenger trains can be run from 60 to 100 miles per hour with safety, upon a well constructed road—an attainment which, with the present arrangement, is impossible.

ORDINARY PASSENGER TRAINS.

By adopting the three-cylinder locomotive, heavier trains than at present used, can be moved with greater regularity of motion, and less wear and tear to the permanent way, than by the ordinary construction.

FREIGHT TRAINS.

The cost of transport of freight may, by the use of the heavy double engine, be reduced one half, while the use of sand for adhesion, the trouble of starting heavy loads, and the evil of grades is almost entirely removed. The power of the new arrangement admits of being applied to a greater or less extent, according to the work to be done. The tractive or adhesive power may be varied at pleasure. By use of the direct blast, combustion may be brought to a maximum when most desired, i. e. on steep inclines. (In the common arrangement, the reverse is the case—the slower the motion the less the blast.) The number of trains may be greatly reduced, and thereby liability to accident, and capital invested in terminal depot arrangements.

I will add a few remarks on the advantage of concentrated power, the use of heavy and less frequent trains upon the leading New England roads, from the American Railroad Journal, and then conclude.

"I have been thus particular in stating the general principles which control the cost of freight transportation, because there are so many roads in New England which stand so palpably in need of their application. A large share of the soundest and most essential capital has been invested in great lines of Railroads aiming to secure a Western business, besides the development of a local trade. These roads have encountered natural difficulties, such as cannot be profitably controlled, except by concentrated power. The cost of moving one train one mile, on the Western road, has averaged 1.4 cent; the charge has been 2.8 cent per mile.

* * * * * *

"It has been the continual effort of those interested in New England roads to devise means for attracting to them the great through business for which the natural water routes, at their western termini, are successful competitors. The only plans that have been urged were the construction of lines with easier grades, less distance, and the adoption of lower charges for freight.

* * * * * *

"By this means more business would offer, and *more* engines, of the present construction, be required to do it. The expenses of working and the receipts would increase nearly in proportion.

* * * * * *

"In the mean time the through business moving eastward on New England roads is rapidly falling off; that of the Western road was but half in 1852 of what it was in 1847.

* * * * * *

"If a road, by a different system of motive power, could operate maximum trains of 100 tons, [and the power of the new engine is 1000,] they might reduce the cost to 1 cent, and the charge to 2 cents per ton per mile. Instead of 28,153,544 tons of freight moved one mile in 1853, 39,310,793 tons could have been moved—an increase of about 40 per cent. With this increase of freight, the road could afford to receive a less proportion of profit on its transportation, by reason of the *travel* which would thereby be attracted.

* * * * * *

"As a necessary and only means of reducing the cost of freight transportation on New England roads, and of arresting the rapid decline of their foreign business, a prompt and judicious application is necessary of the principles of concentration of power."

www.ingramcontent.com/pod-product-compliance
Lightning Source LLC
LaVergne TN
LVHW011141110826
845150LV00008B/2443

* 9 7 8 1 4 1 8 1 9 2 8 0 8 *